THE
DEBT
DENOMINATOR

How to Dig Deep Beyond the Surface
to Divorce Your Debt

IMANI L. HAMILTON

The Debt Denominator
How to Dig Deep Beyond the Surface to Divorce Your Debt

Copyright © 2021 Imani L. Hamilton

All rights reserved. No part of this publication may be reproduced, stored in a retrieval system, or transmitted in any form or by any means: electronic, mechanical, photocopying, recording, or otherwise, without the prior written permission of the publisher, except in the case of brief quotations embodied in critical articles and reviews.

Scripture quotations marked KJV are taken from the King James Version of the Holy Bible, which is in the public domain.

Scripture quotations marked NIV are taken from THE HOLY BIBLE, NEW INTERNATIONAL VERSION®, NIV® Copyright © 1973, 1978, 1984, 2011 by Biblica, Inc.® Used by permission. All rights reserved worldwide.

Scripture quotations marked NLT are taken from the *Holy Bible*, New Living Translation, copyright © 1996, 2004, 2015 by Tyndale House Foundation. Used by permission of Tyndale House Publishers, Inc., Carol Stream, Illinois 60188. All rights reserved.

Scripture quotations marked AMP are taken from the Amplified® Bible (AMP), Copyright © 2015 by The Lockman Foundation. Used by permission. www.lockman.org

Because of the dynamic nature of the Internet, any web addresses or links contained in this book may have changed since publication and may no longer be valid.

ISBN: 978-1-7367666-0-6 (Paperback)
ISBN: 978-1-7367666-1-3 (E-book)

Library of Congress Control Number: 2021906063

Requests for information should be sent to: imani@financebyfaith.com

Printed in the United States of America

CONTENTS

Debt Free Toolkit.. 1
Acknowledgments...................................... 3
Dedication... 5

Introduction... 9

Stand Firm in Faith: The Way Side 21
1 Anchor Your Stance............................... 23

Solidify Your Strategy: Rocky Ground 31
2 Locate Where You Are 33
3 Be Cash Flow Positive 43
4 Maximize Your Cash Flow 51
5 Focus Your Cash Flow 59

Keep Your Eyes Open: Thorny Ground.................. 67
6 Watch for Pitfalls 69

Persevere with Patience: Good Ground 77
7 Stay the Course................................... 79

The Debt Denominator Summary 85
Glossary... 87
Notes 91

DEBT FREE TOOLKIT

Before you begin, I have created a toolkit of templates to help you take action as you move through the book. You can access them for free at www.financebyfaith.com/debt-free-toolkit.

ACKNOWLEDGMENTS

I give honor and glory to God for showing me this path to debt freedom.

To my husband Ross Hamilton, Jr., thank you for always pushing me forward and encouraging me to follow God's leading.

To my mother Dorothy Carn, thank you for your unwavering support and countless hours of wise counsel.

To Nichelle Bennett, Tonisha and Ferris Joanis, thank you for being my first readers and providing such invaluable feedback.

To my father Andrew Carn, cousins and the rest of my family, God outdone himself when he blessed me with each of you. I am ever so grateful for our bond.

Love you all.

DEDICATION

This book is dedicated to my husband Ross and children Anaya, Azaria and Michael. Love you always.

PREFACE

The Debt Denominator is a framework for anyone who desires to get beyond their debt but cannot see a way forward. As I coach clients to help them chart a path toward achieving their financial goals, I discover the common theme that plagues so many is the debt load they carry and the impact it has on their progress to financial independence. Common phrases I hear are, "I'm never going to be able to pay off my debt," or "I'm going to die with my debt." If these statements resonate with you, let me be the first to tell you that you do not have to settle for having debt until you pass from this earth. If you are challenged by that statement, listen to what God has to say about it in Deuteronomy 15:1–2 (NLT):

> "At the end of every seventh year you must cancel the debts of everyone who owes you money. This is how it must be done. Everyone must cancel the loans they have made to their fellow Israelites. They

must not demand payment from their neighbors or relatives, for the LORD's time of release has arrived."

In the Old Testament, the children of Israel were to be set free from bondage and released of all indebtedness every seven years. While this is not a rule today, it shows the heart of God; he did not intend for us to be in debt for a lifetime. My prayer is The Debt Denominator gives you the path you need to move your mountain of debt so you can pursue all that God has promised you.

INTRODUCTION

My Debt Story

I grew up in North Philadelphia in the 1980s and 1990s. It has since experienced gentrification, but during my time there, it had a high concentration of poverty and blight. The block that I grew up on was fully occupied except for two vacant properties that my parents owned. They had every intention of renovating the homes but didn't finish before selling them. Just knowing we owned three properties on one block taught me about the value of property ownership, and I couldn't wait to purchase a place of my own.

My husband and I started investing in real estate in the early 2000s. We were doing pretty well, selling two properties in a few short years at twice the price we paid. Little did I know we were riding a wave and the 2008 Great Recession was on the horizon. When the recession hit, we were stuck with a property we could not sell. We couldn't even get a short sale done, which means we would have sold the property for less than we owed with lender approval. We then tried to rent it, but we had to settle for a monthly rent that was less than the mortgage payments. Plus, the tenant stopped paying after the third month. It was horrible. The housing market was taking an exceptionally long time to recover. Our savings dwindled with each passing month, and eventually our account ran dry. We were ultimately forced to return the property back to the bank through a deed in lieu of foreclosure. This means we agreed to give the keys to the lender to avoid foreclosure proceedings.

Despite the humiliation of losing all we had gained, I learned that I enjoyed real estate and wanted to transition into the industry full time. So, by the time the deed-in-lieu transaction was finally complete, I had just started my first year pursuing my MBA in real estate and finance at The Wharton School, University of Pennsylvania.

I was tormented during that first year. I was at one of the top business schools in the country, with a premier real estate program, and was worried my past setbacks would keep me from getting and excelling in a corporate position. Those doubts turned into lies from the enemy that I had to battle and reject to make it through the program and regain confidence.

Upon graduation, I had the opportunity to join the commercial real estate lending division at a regional bank. This position taught me about the business of debt. My job was to originate loans and manage those relationships—in other words, sell debt to others.

INTRODUCTION

Unfortunately, by the beginning of 2014, having been through the recession, my husband and I were staring at six figures in student loan debt from graduate school and car loan debt. Plus, having been exposed to the other side of the debt table as a lender, I realized my husband and I needed to get out of debt. Proverbs 2:6–7 (KJV) states:

> "For the LORD giveth wisdom: out of his mouth cometh knowledge and understanding. He layeth up sound wisdom for the righteous: he is a buckler to them that walk uprightly."

Within three years and nine months, we were able to pay off those loans, following the steps of The Debt Denominator! Breaking free from debt positions you to confidently say yes to divine opportunities, reclaim your future, and steward God's resources where he wants them to go, for all of it is his.

The Debt Denominator

> *"And God blessed them, and God said unto them, Be fruitful, and multiply, and replenish the earth, and subdue it..."*—Genesis 1:28 (KJV)

In Genesis 1, God gave his first command: be fruitful. Being fruitful means being productive in the things God has called us to do. Given the position God gave it in the Bible (the beginning) being fruitful is not only a priority, but it is also expected as a Kingdom citizen. In order to be fruitful, however, we must meet the condition in John 15:5 (NLT), for Jesus states:

> "Yes, I am the vine; you are the branches. Those who remain in me, and I in them, will produce much fruit. For apart from me you can do nothing."

Every spring I watch my husband prepare the garden for the upcoming season. He waits until the weather gets to a specific temperature, then spends an entire Saturday prepping the ground to receive the seeds he is about to plant. He studies the movement of the sun around the garden and the position of the trees to figure out where to strategically place each vegetable for the best harvest. If he plants too soon or places the vegetables in too much or too little sun, they will not produce their full potential. As a matter of fact, some may not produce anything at all. Conditions matter.

Now you are probably thinking, *That is great, but what in the world does this have to do with getting out of debt?* Everything!

The Debt Denominator is a strategy to debt freedom. If you remember from your fourth-grade math class, the numerator is the part of the fraction above the line, and the denominator is the part of the fraction below the line that represents the full picture. Do not worry; we will not be calculating fractions. The Debt Denominator is a metaphor that represents the conditions that are needed beneath the surface to successfully eliminate the amount that sits above the surface: your debt.

INTRODUCTION

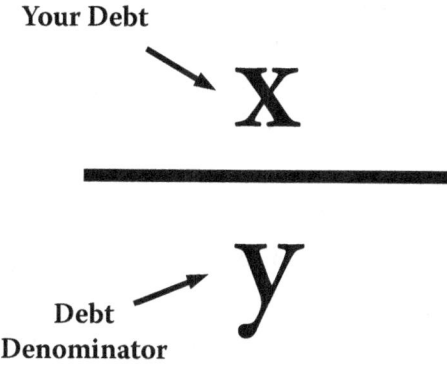

The Debt Denominator framework is a seven-step guide based on the Parable of the Sower found in Matthew 13, Mark 4, and Luke 8. To be clear, the Parable of the Sower is not a text about money. At its core, it is about the gospel of the Kingdom of God breaking into the world.[1] However, its principles provide great insight into a pathway to debt freedom when a financial lens is applied.

The parable describes a farmer who sows seeds in four types of soil. A seed's ability to be fruitful is affected by the conditions of the soil. These conditions provide a blueprint for what it takes to be in good ground and symbolizes what is necessary to become debt free.

Parable of the Sower

In Luke 8:5–15 (KJV), Jesus shares with his disciples the following parable and its meaning:

"A sower went out to sow his seed: and as he sowed, some fell by the way side; and it was trodden down, and the fowls of the air devoured it. And some fell upon a rock; and as soon as it was sprung up, it withered away, because it lacked moisture. And some fell among thorns; and the thorns sprang up with it, and choked it. And other fell on good ground, and sprang up, and bare fruit an hundredfold. And when he had said these things, he cried, He that hath ears to hear, let him hear. And his disciples asked him, saying, What might this parable be? And he said, Unto you it is given to know the mysteries of the kingdom of God: but to others in parables; that seeing they might not see, and hearing they might not understand. Now the parable is this: The seed is the word of God. Those by the way side are they that hear; then cometh the devil, and taketh away the word out of their hearts, lest they should believe and be saved. They on the rock are they, which, when they hear, receive the word with joy; and these have no root, which for a while believe, and in time of temptation fall away. And that which fell among thorns are they, which, when they have heard, go forth, and are choked with cares and riches and pleasures of this life, and bring no fruit to perfection. But that on the good ground are they, which in an honest and good heart, having heard the word, keep it, and bring forth fruit with patience."

INTRODUCTION

A Fruitful Plan

As Jesus explained to his disciples, the seed in the Parable of the Sower represents God's word, while the various conditions of the ground on which the seed fell represent the different responses people who receive the word might have upon hearing it.[1] Of the four conditions described in the parable, only one was fruitful.

While I fully understand the purpose and meaning behind this parable goes deeper than the subject of this book, each section of the book draws parallels from the parable to examine the conditions that affected the fruitfulness of the seed so you can be positioned in good ground to get out of debt. I will go through each condition in depth, but first, here is a brief summary of the four types of soil where the seed fell and the results.

Way Side: Stand firm in faith

Those by the way side were unfruitful. They heard the word but did not believe it because it was snatched out of their hearts. Some families believe they have to live with debt forever because that mindset has been passed down through the generations. Families that have this perspective believe that paying off student loans, cars, and other debt is unheard of. This mindset has been so deeply ingrained into their hearts and lives that they don't believe debt freedom is possible.

In this section, I will cover what the word of God has to say about debt so you will recognize and understand the seed that falls by the way side and how to guard your heart so you can stand firm in faith and be anchored for the road ahead.

Rocky Ground: Solidify your strategy

The seed that fell on rocky ground are those who received the word with joy and sprang up quickly, but they were unfruitful because they were not rooted. The thought of paying off your debt can be exciting, and, in the early stages, that excitement can motivate you to start paying it down aggressively, but if you lack the foundation and a strategy for what to do and when to do it, it is easy to spin your wheels, give up, or accumulate even more debt.

In this section, we are going to cover how to take inventory of your debt, take a pulse of your debt relationship, maximize your cash flow, and develop a focused successful debt-reduction roadmap.

Thorny Ground: Keep your eyes open

The seed that fell on thorny ground represents those who were unfruitful because they were choked by the cares, riches, and pleasures of life. Many influences steer us toward debt. Even if you have a plan and the best of intentions, it can be challenging to follow through with that plan because of external factors and our own internal desires.

In this section, I am going to teach you how to identify the pitfalls to watch out for so you are not blindsided and can stay on track.

INTRODUCTION

Good Ground: Persevere with patience

The seed that fell on the good ground represents those who were fruitful because they anchored themselves in the word, were rooted in strategy, navigated the pitfalls that come with the cares of this life, and let patience have its perfect work. When you are focused, committed, and disciplined, you are positioned to achieve your goals.

Getting out of debt is not a quick sprint. You may be able to get into debt overnight, but you are not going to get out as quickly. In this section, we are going to cover how to stay the course and finish your race. It is worth it!

LET'S DIG DEEPER

Before we move on, let's identify why you want to get out of debt. Getting beyond your debt has both tangible and intangible benefits. Allow yourself to dream. It will be great motivation along your journey.

1) What would you be able to do if you did not have debt?

_____
_____
_____
_____
_____
_____
_____
_____
_____
_____
_____
_____
_____
_____

INTRODUCTION

2) How would you feel knowing you no longer have creditors to pay?

_____
_____
_____
_____
_____
_____
_____
_____
_____
_____
_____
_____
_____
_____
_____
_____
_____
_____
_____
_____

STAND FIRM IN FAITH

THE WAY SIDE

$$\frac{x}{y}$$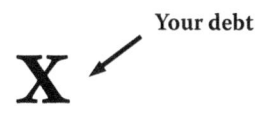

Your debt

- **Anchor your stance**
- Locate where you are
- Be cash flow positive
- Maximize your cash flow
- Focus your cash flow
- Watch for pitfalls
- Stay the course

CHAPTER 1

ANCHOR YOUR STANCE

I was amazed to learn that God has a lot to say about money and debt in his word. As someone who grew up in the church, I was embarrassed that it took me three decades and a financial hardship to see it. Beforehand, when I needed financial direction, I would turn to financial gurus for answers. I don't disavow them, however, because in the multitude of counselors, plans are established (Proverbs 15:22). The problem was I was not seeking the counsel of God, the true financial guru, who was waiting in the wings to reveal his word.

Step #1 of The Debt Denominator is to anchor yourself in God's word concerning your debt-free journey. This is imperative because God is the sower and his word is the seed. You have to know what God's word says about debt and then apply it to your life. Your faith will determine how fruitful you will be in applying his word, and with faith you can move mountains.

> *"So then faith cometh by hearing, and hearing by the word of God."*—Romans 10:17 (KJV)

Knowing the Seed

> *"The rich rule over the poor, and the borrower is slave to the lender."*—Proverbs 22:7 (NIV)

The first time I heard this scripture, I realized I was a slave to my debt. I had lost an investment property in the Great Recession, had over $100,000 in student loan debt, and was therefore unable to pursue certain opportunities.

On two separate occasions I was offered an opportunity to work for companies I loved and with people I cared about, but I had to turn down both jobs because the salaries offered could not support the financial obligations of my debt load. If I had not had all that debt, I would have jumped at both opportunities because the mission behind the work was priceless.

Another biblical reference is in Deuteronomy 28:12 (KJV) where God is talking to the children of Israel about the blessings that would come upon them if they listened diligently to his voice. Included in the myriad of blessings, this scripture declares:

"The LORD shall open unto thee his good treasure, the heaven to give the rain unto thy land in his season, and to bless all the work of thine hand: and thou shalt lend unto many nations, and thou shalt not borrow."

Alternatively, if they did not listen to the voice of the Lord and did not follow his commandments, curses would come upon them. Included in the list of curses, Deuteronomy 28:44 (KJV) declares:

"He shall lend to thee, and thou shalt not lend to him: he shall be the head, and thou shalt be the tail."

While this was an Old Testament covenant, it shows the heart, plan, and vision of God. Debt, financial or otherwise, is not God's best for us as he came to set us free if we heed his voice.

In today's society, it is ostensibly difficult to live without debt. Buying a home without a mortgage is not feasible for most people. The exorbitant cost of a college education has made student loans an almost unavoidable step to getting a degree. Even purchasing a car can be expensive without a loan. But God is the same yesterday, today, and forever, and he does not want us saddled with debt for the length of our days.

Realizing that debt freedom is akin to the fruit, I encourage you to read and meditate on the Parable of the Sower and Deuteronomy 28, and listen to what God has to say concerning your financial situation.

Guarding the Seed

It is important to guard the word you are standing on for your debt-free journey because there is an adversary plotting against you to keep you unfruitful. As we have already surmised from Luke 8, "Those by the way side are they that hear; then cometh the devil, and taketh away the word out of their hearts, lest they should believe and be saved."

The devil wants to fill your mind with doubts that being debt free is possible. He wants you to stay burdened. He wants you to stay bound.

Guard your heart by rejecting doubt, fear, and any other negative messages that arise. Constantly thinking to yourself, *I am going to be in debt forever* does not represent the thoughts of God nor the plans he has for you. 2 Corinthians 10:5 tells us to cast down imaginations and every high thing that exalts itself against the knowledge of God and bring into captivity every thought to the obedience of Christ.

Biblical Affirmations

Here are some affirmations to help you stay anchored in the word concerning your debt:

- I declare that I have the mind of Christ. *(Philippians 2:5)*
- I declare that I am not conformed to this world but transformed by the renewing of my mind. *(Romans 12:2)*

- I declare that I am a lender and not a borrower.
  (Deuteronomy 28:12)
- I declare that I owe no man anything but love; therefore, my debt is paid in full.
  (Romans 13:8)
- I declare the work I use my hands to do will prosper.
  (Psalms 1:3)
- I will not grow weary in well doing.
  (Galatians 6:9)
- I will be content in every situation.
  (Philippians 4:11)
- I will seek first the kingdom of God and his righteousness.
  (Matthew 6:33)
- I will trust God for creative strategies and resources to aid in my debt-free journey.
  (Proverbs 3:5)

LET'S DIG DEEPER

Before we move on, answer the following questions:

1) In the past, what words or thoughts would surface when you thought about your debt?

_____
_____
_____
_____
_____
_____

2) What scripture(s) will you stand on to combat these thoughts?

_____
_____
_____
_____
_____
_____

ANCHOR YOUR STANCE

3) What do you believe is possible about your debt today?

SOLIDIFY YOUR STRATEGY

ROCKY GROUND

$$\frac{x}{y}$$

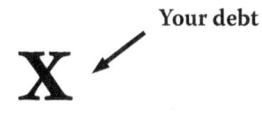 Your debt

- Anchor your stance
- **Locate where you are**
- **Be cash flow positive**
- **Maximize your cash flow**
- **Focus your cash flow**
- Watch for pitfalls
- Stay the course

CHAPTER 2

LOCATE WHERE YOU ARE

I will never forget the day a close friend in a stressed state of mind called me on the phone because her employer's Human Resource Department had just told her that her student loan lender was demanding they be allowed to garnish her wages for defaulting on student loan payments. In other words, the lender wanted to take my friend's monthly loan payment directly out of her paycheck.

Even though my friend had not made any payments on her student loan for years, her company's HR department helped her arrange payments with the lender so that garnishment would not take place. Unfortunately the outstanding balance on her student loan had grown considerably due to years of accrued interest.

If you do not know the amount you owe, the lender you owe, or the terms of your loan payments, paying down your debt can be challenging. I know it is easier to avoid debt out of fear, but I encourage you to face your fears head on, live in your truth, and decide from this day forward that you will not be defeated by debt.

In the Parable of the Sower, the ground was unfruitful because it lacked roots. A primary function of a plant's roots is to provide stability, to fix the plant firmly in the soil for survival. ***Step #2 of The Debt Denominator is to locate where you are.*** Knowing where you are provides a solid foundation, which is critical to arrive at your destination. Have you ever gone to a mall, looking for a particular store, and did not know where it was? To avoid wandering aimlessly, you looked for the closest mall directory, found the store on the map, and located the "you are here" sticker to figure out the most direct path. This step is finding the "you are here" sticker.

> *"The plans of the diligent lead surely to abundance* and *advantage, But everyone who acts in haste comes surely to poverty."*—Proverbs 21:5 (AMP)

Taking Inventory

To locate where you are, take an inventory of your debt and a pulse of your debt relationships. If you have never looked at your loans as relationships, I encourage you to do so. You made a promise and a commitment that binds you and the lender until your final payment. While you're in this committed relationship, your lender can tell you exactly how much you owe and the terms of your obligation.

LOCATE WHERE YOU ARE

As a former commercial real estate lender, I always had the borrower's information at my fingertips, and each loan was formally reviewed every three months. Start gaining control by arming yourself with the same knowledge.

I remember the day I came home to a big surprise. I went to work as usual and took the train home at the end of the day, probably thinking about what my husband and I would have for dinner. I arrived home, put my keys in the door, pushed it open, and was met by a flood of water. There was so much damage I wanted to turn around, shut the door, and forget what I saw. Even though I was afraid to face the devastation, it didn't change the fact that the damage was done, and mildew was beginning to form.

When I walked through my home that day to assess the destruction, I had to make a list of all the items that were affected and indicate which ones were completely unsalvageable. I could not focus solely on what was readily observable on the surface. I had to dig in and open the water-filled drawers and kitchen cabinets in order to capture the full picture.

Debt can cause tons of damage if ignored. You should know the following details about each of your loans:

- ▸ *The original loan balance.* The total principal amount you originally borrowed, whether you borrowed it all at once (as in the case of a car loan or a mortgage) or a little at a time (like a student loan).
- ▸ *The current loan balance.* The total amount you owe today.

- ▸ ***The interest rate and whether it is fixed or variable.*** The cost of borrowing is displayed as an annual percentage of the loan. If your loan's interest rate is variable, your payment can change each month. If your loan has a fixed interest rate, your payment stays the same each month.
- ▸ ***Whether your debt is amortized or interest only.***
- ▸ ***The required monthly payment.*** The amount you are required to pay each month to be considered in good standing with the lender.
- ▸ ***The maturity date of the loan.*** The time period of the loan. It signifies when the loan is required to be paid off or settled, also known as the loan term.
- ▸ ***The name of the lender.*** The person or institution you owe. In the case of student loans, also note which loans are federal (government funded) and which are private.
- ▸ ***The status of your repayment.*** Your loan can either be in repayment, deferred, in forbearance, or in collections.

Check your mailed statements or your online accounts for information on each of your loans. You can also request a credit report, which will provide you with the name of your lender, the status of your loan, the amount of the payment you are required to make each month, the original loan amount, and the current loan amount. Contact your lender to get any additional information.

Under the Fair Credit Reporting Act, you can visit www.annualcreditreport.com to access a free credit report once a year from each of the three credit bureaus: Experian, Equifax, and Transunion. During the COVID-19 pandemic, however, temporary access to free credit reports has been allowed on a weekly basis. Save or print these reports to access later.

The three reports should have the same information, but it is not guaranteed since lenders choose who to report to. This is why you may want to pull all three. Or, you may want to pull just one now to allow you to pull the other reports later in the year without waiting twelve months.

You can also contact the Federal Student Aid Information Center at studentaidhelp.ed.gov to find information on your student loans.

To keep track of your loan details, create a debt schedule to give you a comprehensive overview of all your loans in one place. A sample template is available in the Debt Free Toolkit referenced at the beginning of this book. The template can also be used to calculate your debt-to-income ratio so you will know how much of your income is going toward paying your debt.

To calculate your debt-to-income ratio, divide your total minimum monthly payment by your monthly income. For example, if your monthly debt payments total $500, and your monthly income is $3,000, then your total debt-to-income ratio is $500 / $3000 = 16.7%.

Once you complete your debt schedule, calculate your net worth, which is equal to your assets minus your liabilities. The result determines your wealth at a specific point in time. Assets are the value of what you own, and liabilities (also known as debt) are the current outstanding balances of what you owe.

Assets can include, but are not limited to, the following:

- Cash
- Retirement accounts
- Investment accounts
- Real estate
- Vehicles
- Personal property/items

You can expect your net worth to increase as your debt decreases, assuming everything else stays the same.

Take a Pulse of your Relationships

Now that you have your loan details, take a pulse of your overall relationship with your debts so you can fully understand where you are and where you would like to be.

The Debt Denominator has four primary stages of debt relationships: drowning, treading, swimming, and sailing.

STAGES OF DEBT RELATIONSHIPS

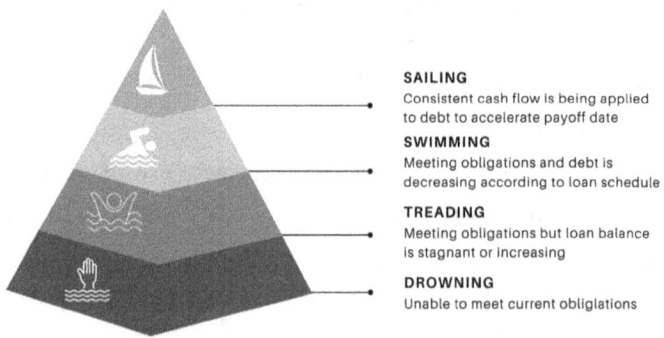

SAILING
Consistent cash flow is being applied to debt to accelerate payoff date

SWIMMING
Meeting obligations and debt is decreasing according to loan schedule

TREADING
Meeting obligations but loan balance is stagnant or increasing

DROWNING
Unable to meet current obligiations

Drowning means you are way over your head in debt, and it is a major cause of stress in your life. You are not able to keep up with your monthly obligations. You have creditors constantly on your back, and you need debt to maintain your lifestyle. You want to meet your payment obligations and become financially stable, but you struggle to get your footing and cannot see your way forward.

If the description of drowning resonates with your current situation, focus on how you can adjust your lifestyle to meet your monthly obligations. The goal is to get all your payment obligations current.

Treading means you can keep up with your monthly obligations, but your debt balances are not decreasing because your required monthly payments are not covering any principal. Your debt may even be increasing if your payments are not enough to cover the accrued interest. If you are treading in your debt, focus on a payment plan that reduces the loan balance each month.

Treading is most common in student loans. Federal student loans allow for affordable repayment plans based on your income but depending on how much you owe and the interest rate, you can be paying an amount that neither covers the principal nor all the interest, which will cause your loan balance to increase with each passing month. The goal is to get your loan balances going in the right direction: Down.

Swimming means your debt load is manageable as long as your income is stable. You are meeting your monthly obligations, and your debt is decreasing according to the loan schedule. It is not decreasing as quickly as you would like, but you know your debt will be paid off at the end of the loan term and has a defined end.

If swimming describes your debt situation, focus on additional cash flow so you can put extra funds toward your debt on a consistent basis and accelerate the paydown process. The goal is to reduce the loan term.

Sailing means your debt load is decreasing at an accelerated rate because you are making extra payments regularly. You may even have assets that are generating enough income to cover your monthly obligations outside of your regular income. You have effectively built a boat to keep you dry.

If sailing describes your situation, you are on your way out. Stay focused on your goal and be open to additional opportunities that can add to your accelerated pace. The goal is to get time.

Whichever stage you find yourself in, be encouraged and know you can be fruitful when you believe in, focus on, and commit to a progressive strategy to pay off your debts.

LOCATE WHERE YOU ARE

LET'S DIG DEEPER

Before we move on, evaluate your debt relationships, complete your debt schedule, and answer the following questions:

1) What is your current relationship with debt?

_____

_____

_____

_____

_____

_____

2) What is your desired relationship with debt?

_____

_____

_____

_____

_____

_____

3) Where do you need to focus to improve your debt relationship?

_____

_____

_____

_____

_____

_____

_____

_____

_____

4) My total debt amount is:

_____

_____

5) My total required monthly payment is:

_____

_____

CHAPTER 3

BE CASH FLOW POSITIVE

There was a time when my husband and I were living comfortably, but we were not free. We both had advanced degrees, we were gainfully employed, we were earning a comfortable household income, and we owned a home in a blue-ribbon school district that our children could benefit from. We were grateful we could afford our lifestyle and pay our bills on time with no problem. However, in reality, we were living paycheck to paycheck because we were not cash flow positive, meaning we did not have a lot of free cash flow.

Free cash flow is the difference between your net income and expenses. It tells you how well you are managing your money and how much you have to work with to pursue financial freedom. Free cash flow may not feel all that important when your focus is comfortability, but when you are focused on becoming financially free, it's everything.

> *"The wise have wealth and luxury, but fools spend whatever they get."*—Proverbs 21:20 (NLT)

As time went on in my corporate career, I became so unfulfilled with my job that my mood would deteriorate on Sunday evenings at the thought of going into the office on Monday morning. I could not just quit my job, though, because we had bills to pay, and we were paying $2700 per month just to remain current on our debt obligations, and that didn't even include the mortgage.

Comfort was no longer good enough. It was time to get free cash flow. Reflecting on the Parable of the Sower, roots absorb water and nutrients for the plant's growth. Consider your free cash flow the nutrients you need to pay down your debt.

Cash Flow Positions

Step #3 of The Debt Denominator is all about being cash flow positive. There are three cash flow positions: cash flow negative, cash flow neutral, and cash flow positive.

Cash flow negative is when your net income is not enough to cover your expenses. When you are in this position, you may feel as though you are drowning because you cannot meet your financial obligations. You may resort to choosing which bills get paid each month (also known as robbing Peter to pay Paul), or you may find yourself in an endless cycle of borrowing to make ends meet.

Cash flow neutral is when your net income is just enough to cover your expenses. In a sense, you are just a middleman, with money passing from one hand to the next, and there is nothing left over for you to pay yourself. When you are in this position, you are treading and comfortable because you can meet your obligations. However, you are stuck and unable to get ahead financially because you have no free cash flow to save, to reduce debt, or to invest.

Cash flow positive is when your net income is more than enough to cover your expenses. This is where you want to be. When you are in this position, you have free cash flow to use to get out of debt faster.

Budgeting for Positive Cash Flow

In order to determine your cash flow position and reach a point of being cash flow positive, develop a household budget. If the thought of a budget feels restrictive, look at it as a plan for your money that you control.

I liken a budget to the weather forecast. Meteorologists study the atmosphere's air pressure, wind gusts, and other factors to predict what the weather conditions will be. We, in turn, use that forecast to plan what transportation we will use to get to work and what type of outfit to wear.

Your budget is a forecast for your money. In it, you detail what you expect your income and expenses to be, based on what you know about your payment obligations and past money habits. Your budget is a powerful asset that is most effective when it is consistently used to guide your financial decisions.

To create a budget, follow this process:

1. Determine the time period.

The time period is the length of time your budget will cover. It can be annually, quarterly, monthly, biweekly, weekly, or daily. For a household, monthly budgets are the most common because most household bills are paid once a month. Annual and quarterly budgets are mostly used by companies. For discussion purposes, a monthly budget will be assumed for the remainder of this book.

2. List your income.

List the monthly dollar amount generated by each income source. Then add all the dollar amounts together to determine your total monthly income. Your budget should focus on your net income, or take-home pay, which is the amount you receive after taxes, and retirement contributions are deducted. It should be the amount you can reliably count on, so consider this, especially if you have incentive or commission income that fluctuates.

Allocate pay periods to the particular month you will use your take-home pay. For example, if you get paid every two weeks and most of your bills are due the first of the month, stagger the paychecks so that the second paycheck from the previous month and the first paycheck from the upcoming month are allocated to the upcoming month's budget.

3. List your bills and regular charitable contributions.

List the amounts of your monthly bills, debt payments, and charitable giving commitments. This can include tithes, housing expenses, utilities, internet, cell phone, insurance, childcare, and student loans. Now you may have some bills, such as insurance, that are paid only once every six months or once a year. If this applies to you, break down that expense into its monthly cost and add it to your budget. Then every month, put that money in a separate account so that when the bill comes due, the money will be there to cover the expense.

4. Other expenses

List your other typical monthly expenses that are not bills. This will include groceries, dry cleaning, eating out, entertainment, and self-care appointments. Then add all the expenses together to calculate your total monthly expenses.

5. Cash flow

Subtract your expenses from your income to determine your cash flow. If your cash flow is above zero, you are cash flow positive. If your cash flow is zero, you are cash flow neutral. If your cash flow is below zero, you are cash flow negative. Being cash flow positive is the overarching goal.

For your budget to be most effective, it should be realistic and your reconciliation systematic so that your chances of following it increases. If you have a family of five, do not budget for a family of two. It may make your cash flow look better, but you will blow your budget every time because it is not sustainable. You may also get annoyed and give up budgeting altogether because it is too restrictive.

Determine how you will document your budget, how often you will compare actual expenditures to what you budgeted, and what day you will commit to reconciling. You can use a budgeting app, spreadsheet, or a pen and paper to document your budget.

After you have created your budget, determine your positive cash flow number because it forces you to be specific about allocating each dollar. Your positive cash flow number is the amount of free cash flow that is consistent every month. This is the amount you can count on and commit to putting to work to reduce your debt. The more positive cash flow you have, the faster you can reduce your debt with the right strategy.

If you are cash flow negative or cash flow neutral, adjust your lifestyle to be cash flow positive. If you are already cash flow positive, congratulations, but do not lock in your cash flow number just yet. Continue reading as we explore ways to increase your positive cash flow number even more.

LET'S DIG DEEPER

Before we move on, determine your cash flow position, create your budget, and answer the following questions:

1) What is your current cash flow position?

_____
_____
_____
_____
_____
_____
_____

2) Would you like to improve your cash flow position?

_____
_____
_____
_____
_____
_____
_____

Budgeting is most effective when you have a system in place to reconcile your budget to actual performance.

3) What budget method will you use to keep track of your finances?

_____
_____
_____
_____
_____
_____

4) How often will you reconcile?

_____
_____
_____

5) What day will you commit to reconciling?

_____
_____
_____

CHAPTER 4

MAXIMIZE YOUR CASH FLOW

After coaching multiple clients, I have learned there is additional cash flow within our reach if we make a self-assessment. I am reminded of a phone call I received from a single mother who was overwhelmed and discouraged with six figures of debt and could not see her way forward. Once I brought up the topic of additional income, she was reminded of a side hustle that at one point had brought in $1,000 per month, but she stopped giving it focus and energy.

Step #4 of The Debt Denominator is to maximize your free cash flow. Cash flow is dependent on two variables: income and expenses. To maximize your positive cash flow, look for ways to maximize your income and minimize your expenses.

Maximizing Income

> "Ship your grain across the sea; after many days you may receive a return. Invest in seven ventures, yes, in eight; you do not know what disaster may come upon the land." —Ecclesiastes 11:1–2 (NIV)

Seek ways to increase your current income, or create other streams of income, using your time, talent, and treasure. There are endless ways to generate income. I will review some of them.

Earned income is the most common form of income. This is the money you earn from giving your time to doing whatever job you are required to perform in exchange for income. This generally requires that you be employed by an entity or a person to perform the required job for an hourly or annual wage.

Consider potential ways to increase your earned income at your current job, and assess your capacity for supplemental part-time employment, even if it is temporary. A good friend of mine took a temporary part-time job just to save for a down payment on a home. Once she accumulated what she needed, she quit the part-time job. You can do the same thing to pay down your debt. Consider it a temporary inconvenience.

Another form of income is business income. This is when you generate income from a business you own. Using your time, talent, knowledge, resources, and influence, you can generate income by creating a product, providing a service, speaking to audiences, referring great products, and attracting advertisement dollars. Most businesses are created to solve problems or meet certain needs, so if you identify a problem or need that you can fulfill, this could be a great opportunity to create a business to generate additional income.

Royalty income is residual income received every time a product you created or helped create is used or sold. If you have an opportunity to be compensated for creating a product, negotiate future royalty income even in lieu of receiving higher upfront fees if it benefits you and if it is a product you believe will have long-term success.

Other types of income such as interest income, dividend income, rental income, and capital gains income can be broadly categorized as investment income and require some upfront capital to make money. These income options are best for those who can afford to take significant risks.

Those who cannot afford to take risks generally put their money toward debt directly, but you might determine whether you have any excess funds available outside of your emergency fund that you can invest in an area where you are knowledgeable and comfortable with the risk.

Interest income is generated by collecting interest on your money. It can be interest collected from money you've deposited at a financial institution, or it can be interest collected from providing a loan. Platforms for peer-to-peer lending would allow you to make loans to others and generate interest income, but they can be very risky.

Dividend income is income received for owning shares of stock in a company that has declared to pay a dividend to its shareholders. Companies who pay dividends announce every quarter how much the dividend per share will be. It is likely that a company that has paid dividends in the past will continue to pay them in the future. Failing to do so would signal to the market that the company is unstable or has financial problems, which could have a significant negative impact on the company's stock price.

Rental income is generated from renting property you own or control to another party. You can purchase a property for the sole purpose of renting it; you can house hack, which means living in a portion of the property you purchased while renting out the remaining portion; or, if you're renting, with the landlord's permission, you can sublet space for more than your current rent.

When renting property, make sure you understand the difference between gross income and net income. Gross income is the amount you expect to receive, while net income is the amount of money left over after property-related expenses are paid.

Capital gains income is generated when you sell an asset for a price that is higher than the price you paid to purchase that asset. It is equal to the difference between the sale price and the purchase price, or your cost basis. This primarily applies to the sale and purchase of stocks, bonds, and real estate.

Minimizing Expenses

The other way to maximize your positive cash flow is to decrease your expenses. When evaluating how to do this, use the RRR approach: reduce, remove, and reevaluate.

MAXIMIZE YOUR CASH FLOW

Reduce: What do you currently use that you can use or consume less? Before I was married and had children, I lived in a one-bedroom apartment. Nine months into the lease, I moved into a studio apartment in the same building, which allowed me to save a couple hundred dollars per month on rent. I was willing to make the temporary sacrifice in order to achieve my goal of saving for a down payment on a home. As a result, I purchased my first home twelve months later. You might also consider switching from premium cable to basic or reduce other discretionary spending.

Remove: What do you currently pay for that you do not use? Categorize each expense as a need or a want and drill into the wants to see if there is anything you can remove. Remember, adjustments made do not have to be permanent. They are just stepping stones to get out of debt so you can be in a better position to live the lifestyle you want.

Reevaluate: What do you currently pay for that you could negotiate a better deal on? One of the biggest areas my husband and I were able to save money on was our insurance policies. If you have insurance on your car or home, you may notice the policies renew automatically, and the premiums may increase at each renewal. After a while, you might find you are paying more than the market price for your policy. That is where we found ourselves. After comparing rates, our annual premium dropped by $1,000.

Another way to accelerate your debt repayment is to renegotiate your interest rates. If you are a homeowner, pay attention to the mortgage interest rates. You may be able to save money by refinancing your home. Loan terms and fees, however, are also important for evaluating a refinance, so talk to a lender and see if this is a potential area of savings for you.

If you have credit card debt, you can request a rate reduction either over the phone or online. There is no secret sauce for a positive response, but if you do not ask, you may not receive it, so ask! A 0% balance transfer credit card may also be a great way to pay down high-interest credit card debt. There is usually an upfront fee, however, so compare the rate after the 0% introductory period to the rate you currently have to figure out what you need to do to make the switch worth your while.

Even though the thought of talking to lenders can be intimidating, get comfortable interacting with them. They are people just like you. Lending institutions are in the business of making money from interest and fees, but their priority is making sure you can pay back what you borrow. If you have a strong credit score, use it to your advantage to get the best terms possible.

Keep in mind you do not have to do it all. Just taking one step to increase your cash flow can go a long way.

LET'S DIG DEEPER

Before we move on, evaluate your income and expenses; then answer the following questions:

1) What ways can you generate additional income using your time, talent, or treasure?

_____
_____
_____
_____
_____
_____
_____

2) What expense(s) can you reduce?

_____
_____
_____
_____
_____
_____
_____

3) What expense(s) can you remove?

_____
_____
_____
_____
_____

4) What expense(s) can you reevaluate?

_____
_____
_____
_____
_____

5) After adjusting your budget, what is your cash flow number (the extra amount you can consistently allocate to paying down your debt each month)?

_____
_____
_____

CHAPTER 5

FOCUS YOUR CASH FLOW

Now that you have established a budget with a consistent positive cash flow number, *Step #5 of The Debt Denominator is to focus your positive cash flow.*

Before we jump into paying down debt, it is important to establish a cash reserve for unexpected emergencies. I remember coming home one day and our garage door had completely snapped. It was so odd that I thought someone may have tried to break in. But after carefully examining the door, it was clear that it really had just broken out of the blue and we had to get it replaced quickly so our personal items would not be exposed.

Sometimes it is hard to predict when "life" will happen and when. Building a cash reserve will help protect your debt-reduction plan once you get started. In the Parable of the Sower, roots serve to store food to nourish the plant in the event of a drought. So, lacking roots, or in this case, savings, could be detrimental if circumstances turn barren.

There are two popular strategies to paying off debt: the debt-snowball method and the debt-avalanche method. While there is a difference between the two, both share one key underlying component: they call for a singular focus on attacking one debt at a time and not allowing for the spread of cash flow around to multiple debts simultaneously. Focus gets the job done.

The Debt-Snowball Method vs. The Avalanche Method

The debt-snowball method requires you to list your debt balances from the lowest dollar amount to the highest dollar amount, then pay the minimum required monthly payment on each of your debts and put any extra money (free cash flow) toward the debt with the lowest balance. Continue to do that until the lowest debt balance is paid off. After this first debt is paid, focus on the second lowest balance by paying the minimum required monthly payment for that debt, PLUS the monthly payment you were making on the first debt, PLUS your original free cash flow. Continue the process until all your debts are paid.

With the debt-avalanche method, list your debts from the one with the highest interest rate to the one with the lowest interest rate. Pay the minimum required monthly payment on each of your debts, and put any extra money (free cash flow) toward the debt with the highest interest rate. Once the first debt is paid off, move your free cash flow and what you were paying on that first debt to the debt with the second highest interest rate until all debts are paid off.

The debt-avalanche method makes the most sense mathematically. If you tackle the debts from the highest interest rate to the lowest, you should pay less interest on your overall debt over time. However, the debt-snowball method makes the most sense psychologically because studies show that people are motivated to keep going and stay the course when they have small wins.[2] We used the snowball method because our higher interest rates were tied to our larger balances, and the quick wins fueled our fire to keep going.

The method you choose will depend on your mix of interest rates and balances and what motivates you to keep going. The only thing that truly matters is that you list your debts in a priority order that best suits you, attack each debt one at a time, and stick with the method until the last debt is paid.

Go back to the debt schedule you created in chapter three and rank your debts in the order you desire to pay them off.

Distance to Payoff

The next step is to calculate how much time it will take to pay off your debts. Taking this step turns your debt-free goal into a SMART goal, which, in the world of strategic problem-solving, stands for specific, measurable, achievable, realistic, and time bound.

THE DEBT DENOMINATOR

Determine the amount of time it will take to pay off the first debt on your priority list. To do this, divide the total amount you owe on your first debt by the expected monthly principal payment for that debt. Remember, if you are paying more than 0% interest on your debt, your monthly payment has a principal balance and an interest rate, so you must break down your total monthly payment to figure out the monthly principal. Once you have done that, add your monthly positive cash flow number to determine the amount of your monthly principal payment. Then divide that number into the amount you owe on your first debt to get the total number of months it will take to pay it off.

On the date your first debt will be paid off, calculate the balance of your second debt. Do the same for each successive debt on your priority list until you have calculated your projected total debt exit date.

Let's assume you owe $2,500 for your first debt. Your monthly payment for that debt is $125. Approximately $25 of it goes to principal and $100 goes to interest. Let's also assume your cash flow number is $75. Add $25 plus $75 to get your monthly principal payment ($100). Then divide that into $2,500 ($2,500 / $100) to get 25 months, which is the amount of time it will take you to pay off your first debt.

If you have a fixed interest rate, your required monthly payments are the same each month, but the interest portion of your payment is decreasing as your outstanding balance is reduced. Therefore, your principal will increase with each payment. This is a feature of an amortizing loan. As a result, in our example, the payoff will likely happen before 25 months.

To tighten your estimate, use an online amortization calculator. You just need to know your original balance, interest rate, and loan term. Extra payments made sooner rather than later will work in your favor to cut down the time to payoff. The sooner you chip away at the principal, the quicker your debt exit will be.

You may feel a little discouraged by the time it will take to pay off your debts, but unexpected money, including tax refunds, bonus pay, and raises, can come your way, and you can use those sources to accelerate the debt-repayment process. When I took these steps and put in the effort to be fruitful, I received unexpected funds that I still cannot explain today. I am a witness that God is able to meet you at your level of faith and bless you beyond what you can imagine.

LET'S DIG DEEPER

Before we move on, evaluate your savings, determine your debt strategy, and then answer the following questions:

1) Are you satisfied with the amount of money in your savings? If not, what is your savings goal?

_____
_____
_____
_____

2) When will you reach your savings goal? Divide your savings goal amount by your cash flow number.

_____
_____
_____
_____
_____
_____
_____

3) Once you have achieved your savings goal, which debt are you going to focus on repaying first?

_____

_____

_____

_____

_____

4) How long will it take you to pay off your first debt?

_____

_____

_____

5) How long will it take you to pay off the total debt you are targeting?

_____

_____

_____

KEEP YOUR EYES OPEN

THORNY GROUND

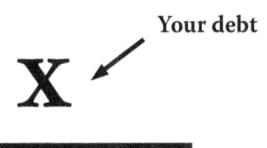

- Anchor your stance
- Locate where you are
- Be cash flow positive
- Maximize your cash flow
- Focus your cash flow
- **Watch for pitfalls**
- Stay the course

CHAPTER 6

WATCH FOR PITFALLS

By this point in The Debt Denominator, you should have completed the following:

1. Anchored yourself in God's word for your journey.
2. Taken inventory and gotten a pulse of your debt relationships.
3. Determined your cash flow position.
4. Maximized your cash flow number.
5. Selected a debt-payoff strategy and made it a SMART goal by focusing your cash flow and calculating your debt-payoff date.

You may be tempted to close the book and run with what you have learned so far, but the next step is just as crucial as the first five. *Step #6 of The Debt Denominator is to watch*

out for pitfalls. In the Parable of the Sower, the seeds that fell on thorny ground were unfruitful because the crop was choked by the cares, riches, and pleasures of this life.

Have you ever made a plan, believed in your plan, was excited about your plan, and yet for some reason did not follow through with your plan? What got in the way? Where did you get stuck? Why did you stumble?

Even with the best of intentions to follow the best plan, getting out of debt is also susceptible to pitfalls. We are marketed, distracted, and tempted to spend money every way we turn. I call these pressure points. Pressure points are items or events that cause your cash flow to go elsewhere instead of toward your debt-free plan, and can cause you to take on additional debt. Taking the time to understand the pressure points that are specific to you will help you learn how to navigate them with confidence. Let's explore these so you are prepared and not blindsided.

Pressure Point #1: Internal Desires

We all have our "thing": shoes, cars, vacations, and lots of other things. But the things you desire come at a cost. Being aware of your weaknesses and how they manifest will help you avoid those desires when you are tempted to fulfill them:

1. Impulse Spending

Impulse spending is purchasing a product or service without allowing time for careful consideration. We are inundated

WATCH FOR PITFALLS

with advertisements for products and services every day. To avoid acting on impulse, give yourself at least a day to think about any purchasing decision. If you decide the purchase is something you need, make room for it in the following month's budget, or save for it.

2. Discounts

A discount is getting something for less than its perceived value. This can mean getting something for 50% off or "buy one get one free." Getting more for your money is an excellent way to make it stretch and a smart way to plan for purchases. However, if the discount causes you to buy something you do not need or would not have bought at its regular price, it becomes a pitfall. Check your finances to see how much you have available to spend on that item, and do not tempt yourself by opening store emails or visiting websites unless you plan to purchase that item in the near term.

3. Status Spending

Have you ever watched HGTV and suddenly had a desire to remodel your kitchen or plan a move? Have you seen people on social media who appear to be living it up, which makes you want to do the same? The old adage of keeping up with the Joneses still exists. When you see the flood of images and videos on social media of people's daily lives, you may be tempted to live beyond what you can comfortably afford. But remember, many people rely on debt to support their lifestyle, so the grass is not always greener on the other side.

4. Emotional Spending

Emotional spending is spending based on the way you feel. Triggers include grief, stress, sadness, and happiness. To avoid emotional spending, find alternative ways to respond to your feelings that do not cost you anything. Consider talking with a trusted person or professional about your emotions to help process your thoughts instead of seeking comfort through spending.

What areas do you need to focus on, and what do you need to watch out for? Where do you get weak? Identifying weaknesses ahead of time will increase your likelihood of staying on track of becoming debt free.

> "Do not conform to the pattern of this world, but be transformed by the renewing of your mind. Then you will be able to test and approve what God's will is—his good, pleasing and perfect will."—Romans 12:2 (NIV)

Pressure Point #2: External Influences

Once I started a banking career, I began to understand the business of debt as a whole and why debt is so prevalent in our lives. Inside the walls of financial institutions, debt is considered a product, and that product is a major source of revenue generated through interest and fees. As such, it is marketed to borrowers like any other product. In fact, marketing debt is so ubiquitous that it is sometimes hard to recognize even when it is staring you in the face. Think about the last car commercial you saw. Do you recall the cost of the car? If you cannot recall, it is likely because the price was not mentioned in the advertisement. Most car commercials highlight the monthly payment to lease or own the vehicle, but rarely do they reveal the price of the car. The advertisement of the car and the advertisement of debt for the car are meshed together. Knowing when and how you are targeted by marketing will increase your chances of resisting the temptation to get into even more debt.

Temptation can be summed up into three categories: 1) lust of the flesh, 2) lust of the eyes, and 3) the pride of life. In Genesis 2, Eve saw that the fruit looked good, it was good to eat, and it would make her wise. All of this tempted her to eat it despite God's instruction not to. The root of temptation has not changed, so watch out.

> *"For all that is in the world, the lust of the flesh, and the lust of the eyes, and the pride of life, is not of the Father, but is of the world."* —1 John 2:16 (KJV)

LET'S DIG DEEPER

Before we move on, answer the following questions:

1) What are your pressure points?

Pressure Point #1:
_____
_____
_____
_____
_____
_____

Pressure Point #2:
_____
_____
_____
_____
_____
_____

WATCH FOR PITFALLS

Pressure Point #3:

_____
_____
_____
_____
_____
_____
_____

2) What mechanism can you put in place to combat these pressure points?

_____
_____
_____
_____
_____
_____
_____
_____
_____

PERSEVERE WITH PATIENCE

GOOD GROUND

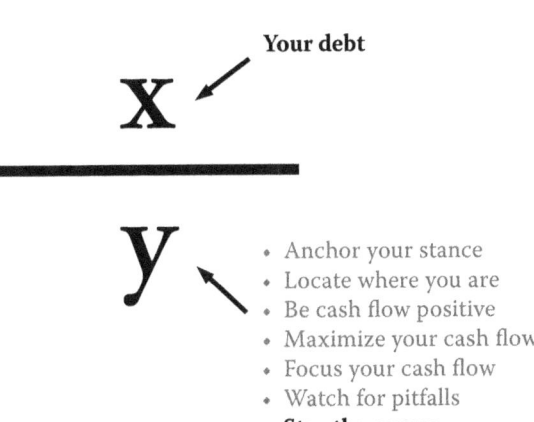

$$\frac{x}{y}$$

x ← Your debt

y
- Anchor your stance
- Locate where you are
- Be cash flow positive
- Maximize your cash flow
- Focus your cash flow
- Watch for pitfalls
- **Stay the course**

CHAPTER 7

STAY THE COURSE

In the Parable of the Sower, the good ground is where the seed was fruitful. It required the conditions not be of the way side, of the rocks, or of the thorns. But it also required an additional condition: patience. **Step #7 of The Debt Denominator is to stay the course with patience.**

> "And let us not be weary in well doing: for in due season we shall reap, if we faint not." —Galatians 6:9 (KJV)

My mother always says, "Patience is a virtue." As you already know from calculating your payoff date, it takes time to get out of debt. While you may have gotten into debt with the stroke of a pen or the click of a button, getting out can take years. The difference in time depends on how much you owe, how much positive cash flow you have available to allocate to debt reduction every month, and whether you stay consistent with your debt-reduction plan. It is a journey, it is a process, and to be successful you must be patient.

Debt Fatigue

At some point during your debt-free journey, you will get tired simply because it takes time. I call this debt fatigue. We live in a culture where everything is quick. If you want a quick meal, just put some food in the microwave and it is ready to go in a few minutes. If you want information, you no longer have to go to the library because the internet is at your fingertips. Communicating with one another via email, text, or direct messaging has conditioned us to seek quick responses, and if your debt paydown is not moving at the same pace, you will be tempted to give up.

We almost did. Our home was built in the 1940s and had not been upgraded, so everything was dated. We decided to prioritize our debts and deal with upgrades later. During our debt-payoff journey, a couple of tiles started to fall off the walls, and the pipes started to rattle if we turned the shower knob past a certain point. I was so fed up and so ready to give up that we called in a few contractors to give us bids. But before we went through with the bathroom renovation, we revisited our projected payoff date, and we were exactly 12 months from being done with our debt goal. So, we stayed the course. It was not fun, but we got it done, and as a result we were able to pay for the renovation in cash.

Motivation

To help you stay motivated, here are some tips:

- Remember your dream. Imagine what you would do with the extra cash flow once your debts are paid off. How would your life be different?
- Celebrate your progress. Paying off your first loan is not only a great feeling, but it is evidence that fuels your momentum to keep going. Whenever you make progress, take a moment to acknowledge and celebrate it. Avoiding temptations is also worthy of acknowledgment because it takes just as much focus and commitment as implementing your plan.
- Be accountable. Find someone you trust to be open and vulnerable with to share your goals and help you stay on track.
- Commit to your future self. If you commit to using your positive cash flow to pay down debt, you will get through your journey.

You Can Do This!

If you made it to the end of the book and completed the action steps, debt freedom can be part of your story. The "forever in debt" generational cycle can end with you. You get to choose. Are you ready?

> *"...I tell you the truth, if you had faith even as small as a mustard seed, you could say to this mountain, 'Move from here to there,' and it would move. Nothing would be impossible."*—Matthew 17:20 (NLT)

STAY THE COURSE

LET'S DIG DEEPER

Before we move on, answer the following questions:

1) Who can you trust to help you stay accountable to your debt-free goals?

_____
_____
_____
_____
_____
_____

2) How will you acknowledge your wins?

_____
_____
_____
_____
_____
_____

3) What will you commit to doing to stay on track?

_____
_____
_____
_____
_____
_____
_____
_____
_____
_____
_____
_____
_____
_____
_____
_____
_____
_____
_____

THE DEBT DENOMINATOR SUMMARY

1. Anchor your stance in God's word concerning your debt-free journey by knowing what the Bible says about debt and guarding that word in your heart.
2. Take inventory of your debt and get a pulse of your debt relationships.
3. Be cash flow positive by developing a realistic budget.
4. Maximize your cash flow number by maximizing your income and minimizing your expenses.
5. Focus your positive cash flow by ranking your debts in the order you will pay each of them off and allocate that cash flow to one debt at a time until all your debts are paid. Also, calculate the total time to payoff.
6. Watch for pitfalls by identifying your pressure points as you work your plan.
7. Stay the course and push through debt fatigue by remaining patient and motivated.

GLOSSARY

Asset: The value of what you own.

Budget: A plan for your money.

Business income: Income generated from a business you own.

Capital gains income: Income generated when you sell an asset for a higher price than you paid to purchase that asset.

Cash flow negative: Your net income is not enough to cover your expenses.

Cash flow neutral: Your net income is just enough to cover your expenses.

Cash flow positive: Your net income is more than enough to cover your expenses.

Current balance: The total amount you owe today.

Deed in lieu of foreclosure: The borrower agrees to transfer the deed to the lender without going through the foreclosure process.

Discount: When you get something for less than its perceived value.

Dividend income: Income received from owning shares of stock in a company that has declared to pay a dividend to its shareholders.

Earned income: Income generated by giving your time to perform a job or task.

Emotional spending: Spending money because of the way you feel.

Fruitful: Being productive in the things God has called you to do.

House hacking: Living in a portion of a property that you own and renting out the remaining portion to another party.

Impulse spending: Purchasing a product or service without giving time for careful consideration.

Interest income: Income generated by collecting interest on your money.

GLOSSARY

Interest rate or APR: The cost of borrowing, displayed as an annual percentage of the loan.

Liabilities: The current outstanding balances of your debt.

Maturity date: The time period of the loan. It signifies when the loan is required to be paid off or settled, also known as the loan term.

Net worth: Assets minus liabilities.

Name of lender: The person or entity you owe. In the case of student loans, note which loans are federal (government funded) and which are private.

Original balance: The total principal amount you originally borrowed, either all at once (as in the case of car loans), or as multiple draws (as in the case of student loans).

Payment status: The status of your repayment. Your loan can either be in repayment, deferred, in forbearance, or collections.

Pressure points: Items or events that would cause your cash flow to go elsewhere or cause you to take on additional debt instead of following your debt-free plan.

Rental income: Income generated from renting property that you own or control to another party.

Required monthly payment: The amount you are required to pay each month to be considered in good standing with the lender.

Royalty income: Residual income received every time a product you created or helped create is used or sold.

Short sale: When the lender approves of the borrower selling the property for less than he or she owes.

Variable or fixed interest rate: If your loan has a variable interest rate, your monthly payment can change each month. If your loan has a fixed interest rate, your monthly payment stays the same each month.

Wage garnishment: When an employer takes the monthly loan payment out of a person's paycheck and pays the lender directly.

NOTES

[1] Carey, Greg. 2019. *Stories Jesus Told: How to Read a Parable.* Nashville: Abingdon Press.

[2] Trudel, Remi. 2016. "Research: The Best Strategy for Paying Off Credit Card Debt." *Harvard Business Review* Digital Articles, December, 2–4.

www.ingramcontent.com/pod-product-compliance
Lightning Source LLC
Chambersburg PA
CBHW070943080526
44589CB00013B/1621